Original title:
Lichen Lessons

Copyright © 2025 Creative Arts Management OÜ
All rights reserved.

Author: Elliot Harrison
ISBN HARDBACK: 978-1-80567-310-1
ISBN PAPERBACK: 978-1-80567-609-6

Life in Inaccessible Places

In crevices high, they find a way,
Tiny beings having a field day.
Clinging to rocks like brave little sprites,
Laughing at folks with their boring heights.

Nature's jesters, bright in their hue,
Stand steadfast while the winds puff and blew.
They shrug off the frost, don't mind the rain,
Happy to bask in their wild terrain.

The Harmony of Old Growth

Old trees chuckle, their wisdom is grand,
With frilly coats, they take a bold stand.
Whispers of ages, not lost on the breeze,
The rustle of leaves is their ticklish tease.

Mossy patches are like old, comfy socks,
Where squirrels can hide or play peek-a-boo mocks.
Each branch overhead sings tales of delight,
In this orchestra, the day's just right.

Interwoven Histories

Here they snuggle, layer on layer,
Ancient stories, oh, what a fairer!
With fables of yore stuck under their skin,
They giggle at time, let the fun begin.

Wrapped up together like tangled old friends,
A party unfurling where laughter transcends.
With every growth ring, a secret to share,
In this tapestry, joy's beyond compare.

Guardians of the Granite

On rugged outcrops, they plant their feet,
Watchers of time, they just can't be beat.
With stubborn resolve and a splash of sass,
They chuckle at climbers, the first and the last.

Cracks are their kingdom, where sunshine peeks,
Whispering secrets in the language of leaks.
They guard the stone with their quirky grace,
In the granite's embrace, a cozy place.

Green Guardians of the Old

On ancient rocks they like to cling,
With colors bright, they dance and sing.
Old trees chuckle in the breeze,
While these tiny pals take life with ease.

They wear a coat of many hues,
With every shade, they never lose.
In rain or shine, they take their stand,
Guardians of the green, oh so grand!

Strange little friends, they laugh and play,
Over mossy stones, they whimsically sway.
In quiet corners where most won't peek,
They share their secrets, giggles at their peak.

So raise a toast to these quirky things,
Nature's jesters with their vibrant wings.
They remind us all, in their funny way,
To enjoy life's mess, come what may!

The Silent Language of Survival

In the quiet of the forest floor,
Two cheeky mates start to explore.
With creeping vines and twists galore,
They whisper secrets we can't ignore.

Ears of the tree can catch their tone,
As they cover bark like fuzzy foam.
Sipping sunlight, they love their space,
Two silly blobs in a warm embrace.

When storms rumble and thunders roll,
They hold on tight; they've got a goal.
With laughter shared in the wild rainfall,
They stick together, never let fall.

Life in the shadows, oh what a shout,
With characters vibrant, there's never a doubt.
Surviving the odds, they're giggling away,
In a world where silliness always can stay!

Chronicles of the Colorful

Once upon an old stone wall,
A riot of colors began to sprawl.
They giggled and jostled, a festival fair,
Making mundane moments a vibrant affair.

With orange patches and greenish lumps,
They tell their stories through wiggles and jumps.
Oh, what a sight in the daylight's gleam!
Nature's own pageant, a riotous dream!

Every crack and crevice holds a tale,
About adventures both small and frail.
Dressed for the party, they never feel shy,
As they leap and twirl 'neath the open sky.

So raise a hand to these vibrant sprites,
With laughter and joy, they brighten our nights.
In the tapestry of life, they're festively bold,
Scribing chronicles loud, uniquely retold!

Verdant Marvels on Ancient Stones

On craggy rocks, they make their bed,
Tiny green hats on a bumpy head.
They wiggle and jiggle in a dance so fine,
Who knew old stones could host such a line?

With patience like turtles in sun's warm glow,
They thrive in a world where few plants can grow.
A symphony played on the hard, cold ground,
Nature's own jesters, never to drown.

Persistence Among the Unforgiving

On my old roof, they sprout with glee,
Against all odds, what a sight to see!
Rain or shine, they don't seem to care,
Planting their flag, they're the ultimate dare.

Blowing winds and the sun's harsh glare,
Yet here they are, boldly standing there.
Nature's comedians, they bravely endure,
With jokes of survival, their hearts are pure.

Whispered Tales of Tenacity

In the silence of woods, they share a tale,
Of sticking around when all hope seems pale.
With a chuckle, they cling to life's rugged art,
Who knew being stubborn could win every heart?

They thrive where nothing else dares to tread,
With a wink to the world, 'No need for dread.'
Each crack of the stone, a stage for their show,
Tiny green jesters putting on a glow.

A Tangle of Life

A riot of colors, a whimsical mess,
On bumpy old surfaces, they love to express.
With gleeful abandon, they entwine and play,
Life's little comedians, brightening the gray.

In a world that keeps turning, they hold their ground,
Invisible threads with each laugh abound.
They teach us in jest, with a smile wide,
In the grand game of life, it's all a fun ride.

Growing Against All Odds

In cracks and crevices, they boldly sprout,
With no light, no care, they twist and twout.
A little green patch, who would ever guess,
They'd thrive in a world requiring finesse.

They dance in the rain, do a silly jig,
While neighbors' gardens are neat and big.
With patience and grit, they cling on tight,
Who knew a small patch could bring such delight?

Beneath the Surface

Under the stones, where the wild things play,
Secrets are whispered at the end of the day.
The layers that hide from the sun's warm kiss,
Hold tales of the world that we cannot miss.

A dance of decay, what a quirky show,
With wiggles and wobbles, they put on a glow.
From damp little nooks, they peek out and grin,
A reminder that life's grand, even in thin.

Unity in Unlikeliness

Two friends in a blob, oh what a sight,
Who knew they could thrive with such pure delight?
One's prickly and rough, the other a fuzz,
Together they flourish, just because!

In spaces where few dare to take a chance,
They bloom with a zest, a peculiar dance.
Yin and yang, they laugh and unite,
In their odd little corner, the world feels just right.

Exploring Textured Teachings

On rocky hillsides, the stories unfold,
Of cozy alliances and friendships bold.
With textures that vary, their lessons abound,
In the craziest places, wisdom is found.

They tickle your toes with their fuzzy embrace,
Teaching us all that there's beauty in grace.
In wobbly formations, they thrive and they cling,
Oh, what a wild joy that unique gives us wing!

Echoes of Adaptation

In a world where weird things thrive,
A fungus dances, keeping alive.
Clinging on rocks, it sings its tune,
Playing hide and seek, under the moon.

It dresses in colors, oh so bright,
A nature's trick, a true delight.
With friends, it sticks, in a playful game,
Sitting in silence, calling each name.

Who knew that moss could get so bold?
With tales of survival waiting to unfold.
Growing on trees, it laughs at the rain,
A cheerful prankster, dancing through pain.

So next time you wander, take a peek,
At these leafy jokers, so unique.
In the cracks of life, they find their way,
Sprinkling joy in a quirky display.

Whispered Wisdom

Underneath the twinkling starry skies,
A wise old moss speaks in sly replies.
"Growing together, that's the key," it said,
"Don't fuss too much, just go ahead!"

With a chuckle, the algae joins the fun,
"We keep it colorful, and we've just begun!"
"A sprinkle of patience, a dash of paste,
We laugh at time; there's never a waste."

Fungi knows best, with a smile so sly,
"Why rush through life? Give slow a try!"
Sticking to surfaces, always in sync,
Pondering life while enjoying a drink.

So gather 'round folks, at dusk and at dawn,
The mossy wise ones have something to fawn.
Learning to adapt with a giggle and cheer,
In the forest's whisper, their wisdom is clear.

The Color of Change

In the forest, hues burst forth, so bold,
Green to gray, and sometimes gold.
A palette of change is nature's game,
Each brushstroke different, yet all the same.

Watch how they mingle, those quirky sprites,
Creating new shades under sunlit lights.
"Blend in or stand out!" they laugh and tease,
In their colorful banter, we find the keys.

Like a chameleon, they switch with glee,
From dull and drab to a vibrant spree.
Nature's own jesters, with colors to share,
Wobbling in wind, as if without care.

The lesson is simple, oh can't you see?
Life's a grand canvas, come paint with me!
Celebrate change in its wild array,
For in every color, there's joy on display.

Sheltering Shadows

In the cool corners where sunlight bends,
Mossy homes are where the fun never ends.
A sanctuary built from whispers and sighs,
With shadows as blankets, beneath the wide skies.

Under old trees, they host a grand feast,
A party of critters, a nature-themed beast.
"Join us!" they call, as they twirl and sway,
In this silly gathering, they laugh and play.

Fungi provide hats, so comfy and round,
A lovely umbrella from the rain hitting the ground.
Sharing their space with a wink and a grin,
In shadowy realms, the wild ones all win.

So when you feel sleepy or lost in your way,
Seek these soft shadows, let laughter hold sway.
In the nooks of the forest, life's cheeky and bright,
With shelters of silliness, oh what a sight!

Green Filaments of Knowledge

In damp corners, they're having a ball,
Clinging to rocks, they seem so small.
Moss and fungi, what a mix!
Nature's own quirky trick.

With vibrant hues, they dance with glee,
Teaching us lessons while we sip our tea.
Who needs a book, just look around,
Wisdom in green, by nature found.

They weather storms, they laugh at rain,
Showing us joy can thrive in pain.
In quiet places, they play and jest,
A reminder that life is a funny quest.

So here's to the ones who cling and grow,
Wise little teachers, don't you know?
In the oddest spots, their secrets lie,
A laugh, a lesson, beneath the sky.

Surviving the Unforgiving

A wall of rock, a barren space,
Yet here they thrive, with style and grace.
No pampered soil, no sunshine bright,
Just grit and guts—what a sight!

Through freezing nights and blazing days,
They find a way in life's wild maze.
With tiny roots, they claim their throne,
A quirky bunch, all on their own.

They chuckle at storms, and hide from the heat,
Resilient little champs, can't be beat.
In this tough world, they teach us well,
To stick around, no matter what befalls.

So raise a glass to the brave and bold,
In a world so harsh, they break the mold.
With roots so small, they stand so proud,
Survivors all, they laugh out loud.

The Tapestry of Toughness

In the wilds where few dare tread,
Colors burst forth from every thread.
A patchwork quilt of colors bright,
A testament to life's stubborn fight.

Nature's artists, without a brush,
Creating beauty in a silent hush.
With every twist, they spin their tale,
Of strength and humor that will not pale.

They cling to places that others flee,
Laughing at challenges, wild and free.
A patch of grit, a splash of cheer,
Their little whispers are always near.

So next time you feel out of place,
Remember their antics, their tenacious grace.
In life's grand play, we all play a part,
A tapestry woven from every heart.

Nature's Antiques

Upon old stones, their stories cling,
Whispers of time, the past they bring.
Like wrinkled folks with tales to share,
Each tiny patch has seen it all—quite rare!

They've weathered ages, storms that brew,
With a chuckle, they spark joy anew.
Faded grandeur in shades of green,
Nature's antiques, so rarely seen.

From dusty ledges, they wave and grin,
Reminding us where we all have been.
In quiet corners, their humor thrives,
A delight that survives through endless jives.

So tip your hat to these timeless beings,
With steadfast charm and endless leanings.
In the museum of nature, they proudly stand,
Old souls with a funny, wise little hand.

Ephemeral Ecosystems

In a world where fungi wear,
Little hats without a care.
Mossy green and funny views,
Dance with sparkle, nature's clues.

They hitch a ride on every tree,
Painting bark like artistry.
A secret laugh, a whisper shared,
Who knew the forest often dared?

In fleeting moments, colors blend,
On nature's whims, we can depend.
Join the cheer and join the fun,
Spores are flying, can't be done!

So if you wander out this way,
Be on the lookout for their play.
A laughing paradise you'll find,
With vibrant jokes that grow entwined.

Underneath the Bark

Underneath where shadows crawl,
Fungus giggles, nature's call.
Silly hats and socks so bright,
Waving hello, what a sight!

They thrive where others might not dare,
Whiskers of green without a care.
Conversations hum on the breeze,
With every sprout, a chuckling tease.

Cracks in the wood hold secrets tight,
Toadstool friends share laughs at night.
Under the bark, a party stirs,
Who knew plants had such funny purrs?

If you lean in and sit real close,
You'd hear the jokes—they love to boast.
Nature's laughter fills the air,
So come and join this silly affair!

Stories in the Cracks

In tiny spaces, tales unwind,
Mossy scribbles, echoes kind.
Cracks tell tales of joy and fear,
Nature's jokes, so loud and clear.

A mushroom sneezes, pollen flies,
Underneath the sleepy skies.
Whispers bounce from roots to leaves,
Telling stories no one believes.

A fairy's dance, a gnome's delight,
Riddles shared under moonlight.
The secrets hide in every gap,
Where Mother Nature lays her map.

With every sprout, a story's spun,
Of happy days and silly fun.
Join in laughter, sing along,
For in those cracks, we all belong!

Adapting Through the Ages

Through ages past, they've made their mark,
In every meadow, every park.
The tricks they use, a sleight of hand,
To thrive in all this lively land.

From rocky cliffs to trees so tall,
Tiny organisms stand up tall.
In every twist, they find a way,
To joke with life, come what may.

With bright green hues, they tease the sun,
In a game where all is fun.
So watch them grow and spread their cheer,
Nature's mischief always near.

Adapting quick, they take their chance,
A wiggle here, a funny dance.
So tip your hat to those so small,
For they stand boldly, amusing all!

Nature's Unyielding Embrace

In the park, a stubborn patch,
Refuses to budge, it's quite the catch.
With each little footstep, it laughs with glee,
Who knew the ground had a sense of spree?

A tree stands tall, flexing its might,
While rocks chuckle softly, out of sheer delight.
Join the party, the plants and I,
We'll dance in the dirt, under the sky.

The grass gives a wink, as if to say,
'Life's like a game, come out and play!'
With roots interwoven, they sing a song,
Of nature's embrace, where we all belong.

So here's to the earth, the joke of it all,
It's the quirkiest party, we're having a ball.
From puddles to petals, we're laughing in style,
In nature's embrace, stay awhile!

The Poetry of Partnership.

Two branches entwined, making a fuss,
Gossiping softly, just us, just us.
'Look at that squirrel, with its acrobatic flair,'
'He thinks he's a star, but he just has no hair!'

The bee buzzes in with a questionable rhyme,
'Is nectar the secret, or just wasting time?'
While ants parade in their tiny parade,
Chanting, 'Teamwork's the trick, we won't be delayed!'

Moss shares a secret, it's rather absurd,
'Even in dampness, it's my time to be heard!'
With fungi chiming in, all giggles and cheer,
'We're all in this together, have a pint of beer?'

In this silly symphony, they find their groove,
With roots interlocked, they constantly move.
The laughter of nature, oh what a delight,
It's a partnership dance, from morning till night!

Mossy Whispers of Resilience

A patch of green grins, what's that you say?
'With patience and humor, I'm here to stay!'
Through rain and through shine, it just doesn't care,
'Join in my party, where worry's a rare!'

Kicking back on a rock, a mossy brigade,
'Growing together, we're not afraid!'
With each little raindrop, they bubble and cheer,
'Life's just a joke, come lend us your ear!'

In the forest's deep shade, fungi join the fun,
'Why be serious? Just enjoy the run!'
With laughter and light, they all take a bow,
'Let's grow even closer, start laughing right now!'

So here in the damp, where the odd mingles well,
Life's simple joy is our favorite spell.
Mossy whispers promise, through thick and through thin,
With a giggle and wiggle, let the fun begin!

Nature's Quiet Teachers.

Under the tree, a lesson unfolds,
In silence so deep, nature's wisdom molds.
'See that old stump with a funny old face?
Life's not a sprint; it's a slow-paced race!'

The leaves chuckle softly, they've got it made,
Blowing in the breeze, like a nature parade.
'If you look at the sky, you'll find a surprise,
Clouds make the silliest of shapes in disguise!'

Roots tangled tightly, a friendship so grand,
Whispered secrets of how to withstand.
'Embrace every bump, every twist and each turn,
In the classroom of life, it's how much you learn!'

So wander the woods, let the wonders be seen,
In each little moment, find the humor between.
Nature, the teacher, with laughter and cheer,
Shows us the fun is always quite near!

The Dance of Decay and Renewal

In the forest, things decay,
But watch them dance the night away.
Moss and mold in a silly spree,
Who knew rot had such energy?

Leaves fall down with a jaunty fling,
Spinning whirls, as if on a swing.
Old trunks laugh with gnarled delight,
While fungi throw a party tonight!

Beneath the loam, it's all a joke,
Each critter dances, no one's woke.
Humor flows in the soggy ground,
In this wild place, fun can be found!

So join the frolic, don't be shy,
Life's a riot as we all comply.
Decay and renewal take the floor,
The forest giggles, can't ignore!

Nature's Hidden Architects

Tiny builders in a mossy hat,
With sticks and stones, they're having a chat.
Their structures cling like they're on a ride,
Nature's architects in the great outside!

With every droplet, life takes flight,
Each little spore aiming for height.
They nudge a rock, and it tries to giggle,
As roots march forth with a wiggly wriggle!

You might not see their master plan,
A rooftop of leaves for each tiny clan.
They gather twigs with a cheeky grin,
Building homes with a little spin!

So next time you stroll beneath the trees,
Remember the builders with such ease.
They might be small, but don't mistake,
These architects know how to shake!

Coexistence beneath the Canopy

A squirrel prances, a bird takes heed,
Sharing snacks like a tasty creed.
Together they laugh, a party of sorts,
Under the canopy, nature's courts.

Mushrooms giggle in a patch of shade,
As insects dance, their dues all paid.
Each gig in the ground—a funny affair,
In this wild world, joy fills the air!

Fungi rooting for the trees so tall,
While flowers bloom to the chirpy call.
Sharing is caring, that's the plan,
As nature whispers, "Let's all be fans!"

Beneath the branches, life's a jest,
Everyone's welcome, no one's a pest!
So tiptoe softly, and join the spree,
Under the leaves, wild and free!

Lessons in Patience

A snail takes its time, not in a rush,
While the hare zooms by with a silly hush.
In slow motion, saplings grow,
As nature teaches the joys of slow.

The wise tortoise sports an easy grin,
While the winds laugh with a playful spin.
In this slow game, time starts to bend,
With every inch gained, it's not the end!

Mushrooms peek from the dampened ground,
Patiently waiting for joy to be found.
Each cozy corner holds its suspense,
In the race of life, it's common sense!

So breathe it in, and take your time,
For every moment holds a rhyme.
In nature's pace, we find our way,
Laughter lingers, come what may!

Partners of Patience

In a world where things move fast,
Growin' slow is a crazy blast.
Nature's glue, a crafty deal,
Sittin' still, what a surreal feel.

With colors that prank the busy bees,
Like old friends under shady trees.
They cling tight through rain and frost,
In this dance, no one gets lost.

Taking bets on who will fade,
As time ticks, this lively trade.
Giggling at the fleeting show,
Here's a lesson, take it slow!

So next time you dash and race,
Remember this little, slow-paced place.
Life can wait; it's not a game,
Partners of patience, not just a name.

Textures of Time

On stony walls, a quirky coat,
A patchwork quilt, with odds to tote.
Each speck a tale from long ago,
Coated in time's silly flow.

Rough edges hug the smoothest stone,
A cozy club where all are known.
Textures dance in light and shade,
In nature's art, absurd arrays made.

Tickling winds that laugh and tease,
Blowing whispers through the trees.
Who knew that life could feel so strange,
Tickling time, a jester's range?

So let's embrace the awkward trails,
Where laughter wraps like fuzzy veils.
Every bump, a story spun,
Textures of time, oh what fun!

The Song of Stone and Skin

Hear that tune beneath the moss?
A melody where stones emboss.
Skin of rock, a serenade,
To join the dance; life's masquerade.

Fumble-dumble, slip and slide,
A rocky waltz, oh what a ride!
Fleshy hues with earthy grace,
Their jive can put a smile on your face.

With every crack and every line,
They tell a joke that's quite divine.
Songs of age in dappled light,
Sing it loud, laugh with delight!

Stone and skin in a whimsy roam,
In nature's choir, they find a home.
Grooving to a funky beat,
In this odd duet, life feels sweet!

Lessons from the Ancient

Old rocks chuckle, wisdom's glee,
In their stillness, secrets we see.
A patch of green, a story spun,
In the past, oh what fun!

With every crack, life's quirks unfold,
Tales of mischief, brave and bold.
Ancient humor in the bark,
Lessons glow like a firefly's spark.

Peeking through a chiseled face,
A snicker waits in nature's space.
What might crumble will surely stand,
It's a silly game, life unplanned.

So let's learn from these wise old pals,
In nature's book, the laughter sprawls.
For every wrinkle on a stone,
Spark joy and giggles, never alone!

The Resilient Veil

In shadows where the moss does cling,
A busy little kingdom springs.
With patience, they create their home,
On rocks and trees, they love to roam.

They dance in rain, they bask in sun,
Two partners, always having fun.
In colors bright, they won't be shy,
Chasing clouds that float on high.

With scraggly hair and dotty spots,
They thrive in all the ugliest plots.
A lesson learned from sprightly cheer,
Embrace the gloom, it's nothing to fear!

Each tiny spore, a little stir,
To little worlds that begin to purr.
In every crack, they find a way,
Laughing as they seize the day.

Home Among the Inhospitable

On barren rocks, they plop and splash,
In harshest winds, they wave and dash.
Where life seems hard, they plant their feet,
In nature's face, they drop a beat.

Oh, how they giggle in the breeze,
With itchy spots and bending knees!
Not much to lose, they take the chance,
In hostile lands, they firmly prance.

Through prickly times, they just don't care,
With wispy roots, they fill the air.
In every nook, a comfy couch,
Full of joy, they're quite the slouch.

They tease the storms, they love the night,
In places dark, they spread their light.
A cozy home, where few would stay,
With chuckles soft, they claim their sway.

Brick by Brick

Layer by layer, they start to bloom,
On crags and walls, they make their room.
With every blip, a structure grows,
The smallest fellows with grand shows.

They'll wedge between the cold hard stone,
In ribbed old bricks, they carve their throne.
With giggles bright, they make it stick,
A little patch, built brick by brick.

When asked their secret, they laugh and say,
"It's not the ground! It's how we play!"
With tiniest hands, they grasp and cling,
In dingy places, they make hearts sing.

They poke through cracks, they celebrate,
In gardens wild, they dance, they mate.
With every whim, they build anew,
A castle grand, with fun as glue!

Spore by Spore

Oh, tiny bits that float in air,
They've packed their bags without a care.
In gusts of laughter, they take flight,
Every journey a new delight.

Scattering joy from bush to tree,
A merry band of wild decree.
With breezy breeches, they dart around,
In every corner, giggles abound.

Wherever they land, they make a scene,
On little sprouts, they paint it green.
With sticky sticks and swirly twist,
In each wild place, they can't resist.

When one drops near, a party starts,
In merry clusters, they share their arts.
These tiny spores, with vibrant glee,
Create a world where fun's the key!

Colonizers of the Threshold

In every crevice, they make a pact,
With nature's whim and a little tact.
On doors left cracked, they boldly slide,
Cheeky little critters, full of pride.

They greet the sun with funky flair,
No space too small, they'll take their share.
A little dash of random spritz,
Bringing life to the strangest bits.

With tiny spoons, they scoop out joy,
Each new invasion, a funky ploy.
On rusty gates and garden walls,
These little jesters have a ball!

To those who scoff and turn away,
They just laugh loud and softly sway.
For in the cracks, they see the gold,
A kingdom bright, where mirth is bold!

Secrets in Stillness

In corners where the shadows play,
Tiny dwellers have their say.
A whisper of green on a cracked wall,
They giggle as they stand tall.

With patience, they cling and wait,
Understanding that slow is fate.
A wink from the breeze, they give a cheer,
"We're here for the party, come grab a beer!"

When the sun shines just right,
They bask in the golden light.
With each raindrop, they throw delight,
"We're just tiny folks, but we feel alright!"

So let's toast to the art of chill,
For even the quiet can have a thrill.
In the silence, laughter spreads,
Life's secrets hide where stillness treads.

The Dance of Survival

In the cracks of the bustling street,
A party's brewing at their feet.
Twists and turns, they twist their stems,
Raise a toast with whimsical gems!

With shoes made of moss, they leap and spin,
Who knew the fun was under our skin?
A tango of green with a dash of gray,
Come join the dance, don't delay!

They know how to cling and swing,
In every wind, they dance and sing.
From rooftops to rocks, what a sight,
Party like it's always night!

So here's to those brave and bold,
In the cracks, their stories unfold.
Let's join the jest, take a chance,
And leave behind a laughter-laden dance!

Shadows on Stone

On old rocks, there's a tale to spin,
Of the tiny creepers, where fun begins.
Casting shadows, they play a game,
In the grand vignette, they make their name.

A hop, skip, jump, and here's a peek,
Watch them in silence, no need to speak.
With sun-kissed backs, they pose on stone,
"We're the kings of this kingdom, all alone!"

Their laughter echoes in the air,
Inudating humor, everywhere.
In the world of the small, joy reigns supreme,
In every shadow, they dare to dream!

So let them frolic, let them thrive,
In every nook, they come alive.
Just a glance at the ground below,
And you'll find a show worth running to know!

Textures of Resilience

On every wall, a quilt is sewn,
With colors bright, they're never alone.
A patchwork life, soft yet bold,
Stories of warmth in the cold.

With a heavy breeze, they don't just sway,
Little fighters, come what may.
In the harshest storms, they laugh and cheer,
"We're cozy here, there's nothing to fear!"

Stickers of life in every hue,
Feels like dancing, all brand new.
A quilt of dreams on nature's skin,
Making the mundane feel like a win!

So raise a glass to the mighty small,
In resilience, they stand tall.
For in every crack, joy can reside,
Let's live like them, full of pride!

Threads of Time and Texture

In cracks and crevices they thrive,
Old friends in nature's jive.
A party hosted by the stone,
With guests who never feel alone.

They twist and tangle on the walls,
Like little clowns at nature's halls.
Sprouting stories, weaving tales,
In vibrant hues, like tiny whales.

The wind might poke, the sun will tease,
But they stand firm with such great ease.
Each day a prank, a giggly plot,
In nature's dance, they tie the knot.

Unraveled secrets on display,
As laughter echoes day by day.
They teach us all to take a chance,
And join in on this silly dance.

Clusters of Wisdom

In corners dark where few will tread,
They gather round on nature's bed.
Whispering secrets in the night,
Sprouting wisdom, what a sight!

They mix and mingle, chat and tease,
Advising rocks on how to freeze.
A summit held right underfoot,
With snacks of earth and roots to loot.

Olden tales of weathered lore,
Shared beneath the ancient door.
With every color, every hue,
They're wise, but oh, so funny too!

Their voices rise in merry cheer,
As they gossip, loud and clear.
These quirky bunch teach all they find,
That wisdom laughs, and so must mind.

Between Rock and a Soft Place

Tucked in tight, between the cracks,
They giggle at the silent lacks.
A cozy nook wheres fun takes root,
As they make life a daily hoot.

Soft and bold, they hold their ground,
In a cushiony space, joy is found.
With fashion sense of green and gray,
They shimmy and shake in a carefree way.

Beneath the weight, they rise and shine,
Like jesters in a rock-bound shrine.
A little humor, not a care,
As they bloom wild, without a scare.

They whisper jokes to every stone,
In the quiet, never alone.
Between the tough and silky soft,
Their laughter lifts us, and it's oft.

Harmonies of Surface and Substance

On rocky canvases, they play,
Crafting tunes in a quirky way.
A symphony of greens and browns,
With giggles echoing through the towns.

Each breath they take brings forth a song,
Where surfaces meet, they dance along.
With substance rich and laughter bright,
They paint the world in pure delight.

In rhythm with the sun and rain,
Their wild antics, oh, what a gain!
Joining nature in this jest,
Each little patch, a vibrant fest.

From spongy beds to rocky halls,
They sing the tales of the Earth's calls.
In every crevice, every spot,
They share their humor, thanks a lot!

Echoes of Endurance

On a rock where no one goes,
Two tiny friends in silence doze.
They wave hello to passing ants,
And giggle loud at mushroom pants.

When the rain makes them all wet,
They dance like fools, without a fret.
Their secret party—none can see,
Just two algae living wild and free.

With sun above and moss below,
They laugh at life, putting on a show.
Always resilient, giving it a whirl,
Who knew the rock held such a world?

In their little patch of gray,
They play their games, come what may.
Endurance looks so silly here,
A comic stretch for all to cheer!

Resilience in the Ruin

In the ruins where no one strolls,
You find the bravest little souls.
With a giggle and a grin so wide,
They climb the stones with laugh and pride.

A crumbling wall—a perfect slide,
They surf on moss, what a fun ride!
With nature's glue, they stick around,
Making the best of broken ground.

Their happy faces—green and spry,
Grow where humans might just sigh.
In the rubble, they swish and sway,
Dancing on ruin, come what may.

Resilience isn't about being tough,
But knowing when to play and bluff.
These little champs, under the sun,
Show us that life can still be fun!

Shadows and Light in Balance

In the shadows where light's a tease,
A party blooms among the trees.
With dappled sunlight, they seek their chance,
These tiny beings love to dance.

Whispers of wind tickle their skin,
In the balance, they find their grin.
They take turns hiding, then pop in sight,
Creating laughter from day to night.

In the light, they shimmer and gleam,
In the dark, they plot the next dream.
Who knew that dark could be so bright,
These tiny tricksters bring sheer delight?

With shadows playing tag around,
They giggle loud—a joyous sound.
In every corner, joy's a rule,
Playing hide and seek's delightfully cool!

The Threads of Survival

On the wind-swept edge of life's great thread,
Two little pals dance without dread.
A tapestry rare, they weave and spin,
With humor and heart, they begin.

With every challenge that comes their way,
They twirl and whirl—come what may.
A woven friendship, oh so bright,
Knits together day and night.

Through storms they laugh, through sun they cheer,
What's a small storm to those who steer?
With threads of gold and laughter spun,
Their survival's just a ton of fun.

So here's the tale of threads so fine,
Stitched with giggles, every line.
In the fabric of nature, a lesson found,
That joy in survival can astound!

Nature's Resilient Palette

In the cracks of an old stone wall,
Colorful patches have a ball.
They dance in the sunlight's glow,
A funny show, don't you know?

With friends like these, life's a blast,
Creating art, they're unsurpassed.
Who needs canvas, brush, or paint?
These quirky bits are heaven's saint!

Each little speck, a bold surprise,
Hiding secrets beneath bright skies.
They chirp, they laugh, never frown,
In nature's hues, they wear the crown!

So here's to growth that's quite absurd,
Teaching patience without a word.
In every nook, they find their place,
Leaving smiles on nature's face.

Finding Beauty in Hard Places

On rocky ledges where few can cling,
Life blooms boldly, a tiny spring.
In cracks and scraps, they stake a claim,
It's a giggle-worthy little game!

With grit and grace, they sure prevail,
Spreading joy, they cannot fail.
They say, 'Look at us, we're here to stay!'
In dormant dreams, they find their way.

Amidst the rubble and the tough,
They show that life can be quite rough.
But every struggle bears a grin,
In every gap, new life begins!

So tip your hat to the unseen crew,
Who thrive in spaces we never knew.
In beauty's name, they shout and cheer,
Their tenacity, let's hold dear!

The Geometry of Growth

In angular shapes, they twist and turn,
Making diagrams that brightly burn.
With pointed edges, vibrant shows,
They defy logic, strike funny poses!

Calculating how they can spread,
In squiggly lines, their art misled.
A chart of laughs, they draw with flair,
In the wild math, they don't care!

Nature's math has its own style,
Making patterns that make us smile.
From circles small to spirals wide,
They turn growth into a funny ride!

So next time you spot a patch so bright,
Remember, it's life's quirky light.
In shapes and forms, they come alive,
Math so wacky, it helps us thrive!

Lessons in Layered Lives

In layers thick, their stories weave,
Like lasagna, they aim to please.
Beneath the surface, lives collide,
They laugh and play, no need to hide!

Each layer tells a tale so bold,
Of sun and shade, of warmth and cold.
They hoot and holler, a hidden thrill,
In every fold, new lessons spill!

So lift the layers, take a peek,
Find treasures where it's grim and bleak.
In every stack, there's joy to find,
A lesson wrapped, uniquely designed!

So here's to layers, thick and thin,
To funny tales that make us grin.
In nature's depths, they teach and play,
Layered wisdom, brightening our day!

Fragile Foundations

On stones we cling with all our might,
A patchwork green, a silly sight.
We dance in rain, we laugh in sun,
Who knew life's humor could be this fun?

We wiggle close, avoid the fall,
Each tiny step, a quirky crawl.
In windy gusts we hold our breath,
Embracing life, defying death.

Our roots are small, yet dreams are grand,
Together we thrive, hand in hand.
Like comic strips on nature's page,
With every squabble, we engage.

When storms arrive, we play our game,
What's falling down brings us no shame.
We'll patch it up, make it a show,
In this old world, we're the stars, you know!

The Alchemy of Moss

In shady spots where secrets brew,
A fuzzy cloak of vibrant hue.
We sip the dew, we share a laugh,
Crafting a world from nature's half.

A chemistry of slime and cheer,
Transmuting gloom, we disappear.
With every squish beneath our feet,
We find a rhythm, a pulsing beat.

We gather light, a glittering stash,
Turning the mundane into a splash.
In our own way, we're quite the wizards,
With fun concoctions that spark with blizzards.

In this green maze, absurd we prance,
In every spore, we take a chance.
Joy in the chaos, a playful toss,
Behold the magic of mossy gloss!

Intertwined Journeys

Two strands of fate, we twine and weave,
Through cracks and crevices, we believe.
A flirt with fate, a brazen groove,
In every twist, we find our move.

We grow like gossip, as wild as dreams,
At each sharp corner, life's bursting seams.
Kissing the wind, we shout out loud,
In this tangled world, we're ever proud.

The longer we cling, the wilder it gets,
With every surprise, we place our bets.
In this green dance, there's laughter to find,
Two threads of wonder, beautifully blind!

Our journeys interlace, a grand parade,
In every corner, shadows invade.
But with bright colors, we stride with flair,
In our tempest dance, we conquer despair!

Secrets of the Rock

Underneath where whispers dwell,
We's contrived a tale to tell.
Secrets hidden, snug and tight,
We giggle softly, in the night.

In every crevice, clues await,
A quiet laugh, our silly fate.
With pebbled paths and sticky ends,
Nature's puzzles always bends.

We gather close like gossipy friends,
To share the word till daylight ends.
What's boring stone becomes a stage,
Our antics bursting from the page.

The secrets shared with every crack,
Turn solid stone to a wacky track.
In rocky arms, we take a chance,
Like jester's jive in a mossy dance!

Stories Written in Crystals

In the stone, stories unfold,
Tiny tales, both shy and bold.
A frog once tried to sing a tune,
But slipped and fell beneath the moon.

Mushrooms giggle, dancing nearby,
As ants march by, oh so spry.
A pearl of wisdom on a twig,
Tells stories that simply wig.

The crystals hold a party grand,
With beetles tapping, all well planned.
A snail brings snacks, oh what a feast!
While spiders weave, the show's a beast!

So next time you're beneath a tree,
Listen close, and you might see,
The crystal tales that come to life,
Amidst the chuckles and the strife.

The Hidden Life Above Ground

Beneath the grass, a world so sly,
A beetle dons a tie and bow, oh my!
While worms exchange the latest news,
And caterpillars read the blues.

Frogs in tuxedos hop with flair,
While crickets strut without a care.
Butterflies, they sip on tea,
In this garden jubilee.

The hidden ones put on a show,
With acorns holding hands, you know.
A chubby squirrel joins the fun,
With a belly laugh and a nutty pun.

So peek beneath the leafy scenes,
And join their playful, silly schemes.
In nature's party, all are crowned,
In the hidden life above the ground.

Sketches on Solid Ground

On solid ground, the pencils play,
With squiggles bright, in a wild array.
Roots draw lines that twist and twine,
While ants make paths, each one divine.

A dandelion sketches in the air,
While clovers laugh without a care.
A ladybug paints with shiny spots,
Creating works that tie up knots.

The rocks, they summarize the day,
While stones debate the best display.
A twig's perspective makes it clear,
That creativity can bring a cheer!

So grab a brush, let loose your grin,
And sketch away—let the fun begin!
On solid ground, with joy, we're bound,
In nature's art, pure laughter found.

Adapting in Stillness

In quiet corners, life resides,
Adapting softly, where humor hides.
A snail wears shades, quite low-key,
While mushrooms giggle, oh so free.

A rock with wisdom, cracked and worn,
Shares jokes with moss, bright and adorned.
The wind joins in, a gentle tease,
As nature dances with perfect ease.

Fungi fashion hats out of dew,
And critters plot in shades of blue.
With clever minds and giggling hearts,
They master stillness, a work of arts.

So pause awhile, and join the play,
In adapting stillness, we find our way.
With laughter echoing all around,
In nature's wisdom, joy is found.

Life Clinging to the Edge

On stones they stick, a tenacious clan,
With the slightest breeze, they make a plan.
Daring to live where most would not dare,
They laugh in the wind, with none to care.

In colors bright, a twist of fate,
With each little drop, they celebrate.
A party on rock, a whimsical scene,
Nature's own jesters, proud and serene.

Through rain and shine, they never relent,
A comedy act, with no need to vent.
A dash of green, a hint of gray,
Together they thrive, in their quirky way.

Salt of the earth, but with humor so bold,
Each little patch has a story untold.
Clinging with gusto, they sing a sweet tune,
A riotous life, beneath the moon.

Growth on the Brink

On the edge of fate, they cling and thrive,
In a world so tough, they still arrive.
With a stretch and a giggle, they find their zone,
An accidental patch, now happily grown.

Bouncing on rocks, they hold a grand show,
Making a home where no one would go.
They tickle the stones with each tiny sprout,
A show of sheer will, there's no doubt!

Cheerful green blobs in a rocky parade,
Convinced they're the stars in this curious charade.
Whispering secrets to the old mountain's face,
They dance in the wind, with such charming grace.

In the face of great odds, they make a bold stand,
With laughter and style, they grow hand in hand.
To edges of life, with joy they cling,
A brave little troupe, always ready to sing.

The Color of Cooperation

In shades of green, they pull together,
Creating a quilt in all kinds of weather.
One tiny patch, then two, then three,
A colorful mob, as bright as can be!

They share their space, with no hint of spite,
A riot of colors, a whimsical sight.
Whispering secrets, they giggle and grow,
Each little ally with stories to show.

A tapestry stitched from rock to rock,
Their playful antics startle the clock.
In a world full of rules, they find their own way,
Making the mundane a vibrant display!

Together they flourish, a jolly brigade,
Cooperating softly, a life well-made.
With a mixture of hues, they weave and they play,
Nature's own jesters in a grand cabaret.

A Symphony of Survival

In a silent world, they throw a loud show,
With colors of courage that ebb and flow.
A band of outliers, a quirky delight,
Playing their tune in the shadowy light.

With rhythm and style, they cling to their place,
Each note a reminder, life's a wild race.
They dance on the edge, a fanciful spree,
Crafting a ballad of harmony.

Each droplet of rain is a song they adore,
A vivacious chorus that begs for encore.
With every small gust, they sway and they lead,
In a jam with nature, they inspire with speed.

From stone to stone, they make their own way,
Creating a symphony, come what may.
With laughter and light, they teach us to thrive,
In a world full of wonder, keep the song alive!

Unseen Ties

In cracks of stone, they take their stand,
A greenish friend, both stout and bland.
They hug the walls, quite close, you see,
A silent pact of company.

With no phone plans, they chat away,
Sharing gossip of the day.
Their little world, a cozy nook,
In every crevice, a living book.

As raindrops fall, they cheer and sway,
Throwing parties in disarray.
With no RSVP, they dress real nice,
In funky hues, they roll the dice.

So here's to bonds that rarely fade,
In nature's waltz, they're never frayed.
Invisible threads that interlace,
A jolly crew, a funny place.

Growth in Harmony

Two old pals on a rocky ledge,
Share a laugh near the water's edge.
They grow together, a perfect team,
In this wild world, they always beam.

One's a fluffy moss, bright and bold,
The other, a crust, shy yet old.
"Let's take selfies!" one cheekily said,
"Being this cute, we can't be misread!"

With sunlight's kiss, they sway in glee,
Living life, carefree and free.
In every crack, they raise a toast,
To awkward blooms and a grand host.

Through every storm, they hold on tight,
A comical duo, quite the sight.
In laughter's laps, they twist and twine,
A quirky thread of nature's design.

Silent Conversations

On weathered stone, they sit and chat,
Without a sound, just imagine that!
One whispers tales of the mountain's past,
While others giggle, oh, what a blast!

They paint the town in shades of green,
With sprightly voices, rarely seen.
"Did you hear what the puddle said?"
"Water is life, and we're well-fed!"

Their secret language drifts and flows,
In every gust, their laughter grows.
With playful jests, they twist and turn,
In their own world, there's much to learn.

So here's to whispers on the breeze,
In strange locations, growing with ease.
With every chuckle, they light the day,
Charming nature in their own way.

Clinging to Time

With ancient roots, they cling with pride,
To surfaces where secrets hide.
Once a sprout, now a sage so wise,
They laugh at time through all the skies.

In winter ice or summer glow,
They play the slow game, and oh, they know!
"Let's take it easy, there's no rush,"
In a world that's fast, they never hush.

A secret dance, so full of grace,
Two little pals in their funny space.
While others rush to chase the clock,
They sip their tea on the old rock.

So here's to the ones who know the score,
In a timeless world, they seek no more.
With giggles shared, they've made a pact,
To cling to moments, and that's a fact.

Patterns of Persistence

On rocks they cling, with all their might,
Colors clash, a peculiar sight.
Eager spores dance with the breeze,
In their world, they do as they please.

They weather storms, they wave at frost,
A tiny army, never lost.
Pollution's kiss, they take in stride,
In the chaos, they find their pride.

From crunchy soups to dinosaur tales,
They laugh at time, while others pale.
Though never flashy, they hold their ground,
In every corner of life, there's sound.

With patience rooted deep and wide,
Lessons gleaned from nature's glide.
So here's to those who greet each day,
In quirky ways, they show the way.

Embracing the Unlikely

Who knew this patch could burst with glee?
A speck of green on a random tree.
It laughs at mold, it mocks decay,
A little rebel in a dull ballet.

Atop iron gates and sidewalk cracks,
It flourishes where most lack.
In the oddest spots, it finds a home,
A funky party, no need to roam.

With nature's glue, it sticks like tape,
Creating art, a vibrant cape.
With every hue, it reigns supreme,
In the surreal, it chases dreams.

So when you feel like you can't belong,
Think of the brave, who sing their song.
Life's unpredictable, laughter's the key,
Join the wild, come dance with glee!

The Breath of the Forgotten

In hidden crevices, secrets lie,
Whispering tales as passersby.
A joke shared with the crumbling wall,
Unexpected friends who never call.

They feast on secrets, cracks, and grime,
Turning decay into rhythm and rhyme.
They nod through winds, they breathe with ease,
Cackling softly like old trees.

With every breath, they spark surprise,
Recalling laughter, the lows and highs.
Chaos lurks, but they thrive well,
In silent stories, their secrets swell.

So when you think all's lost for good,
Just peek where the wild things stood.
For in the cracks, life's jesters play,
While you forget, they're here to stay.

Nature's Timekeepers

Tick-tock goes the time, oh so slow,
Yet underfoot, the stubborn glow.
Mossy carpets on ancient stones,
Histories told in hushed moans.

With seasons changing, making their rounds,
They laugh at clocks and measuring bounds.
They revel in sun and dance in rain,
A giggle here, a joyful strain.

They gather tales from every dawn,
While giants above just yawn and fawn.
The whispers of ages, so sweetly spun,
In tangled threads, they find their fun.

So next time you glance at the ticking face,
Remember the small ones in their wild place.
For in nature's riddle, time finds its grace,
It's often the quirkiest who win the race.

Nature's Quiet Companions

On rocks they cling and laugh away,
Dancing with moss in a green ballet.
They whisper secrets from dusk till dawn,
While squirrels scratch their heads, confused and drawn.

A sunbeam's touch brings them all delight,
In the garden of shadows, they're quite the sight.
They chat with raindrops as they slide,
In the quirky world where nature takes pride.

Resilience in the Shadows

In hidden nooks they start their show,
With patience like pros, they really know.
While others may fidget, fret, and strain,
They sip on sunshine, ignoring the rain.

With every crack and cranny they find,
A half-hearted pun that's one of a kind.
They laugh at storms, then quietly grow,
While the world rushes by, moving fast and slow.

The Wisdom of Ancient Growth

Beneath the trees, they spin their tales,
In hues of green with smart little quails.
With each old bark, there's much to unveil,
While the squirrels, in suits, counter their sales.

Moss and friends throw a party at dawn,
They sip on dew, while the wind plays a song.
"Who needs a map?" they chuckle and say,
"We've been around longer, what's lost is our way!"

Crumbled Ceilings and New Roots

Where ceilings fall, they make a nook,
With roots so clever, they're in every book.
They'll tell you tales of the best of times,
While jumping jacks nearby set off some chimes.

Dust bunnies giggle, as they roam around,
With every tumble, new friendships abound.
In the cracks of chaos, they've made a throne,
An empire of green where the wild weeds have grown.

Secrets of the Stone-Settled

On rocks they wiggle, a secret dance,
Flashing colors in nature's expanse.
Grinning at moss, they start a debate,
Who grows the fluffiest, who can't be late?

A pebble is home, a fortress quite grand,
With roots as their army, they take a stand.
Each tiny speck shows off its own style,
Claiming the spotlight, each grows with a smile.

With weathered faces, they whisper and tease,
Avoiding the rain with extravagant ease.
Competition is fierce, but laughter they share,
In this stony world, nothing's unfair!

So next time you wander where the wild grows,
Remember the secrets the rocky crew knows.
With a wink and a nudge, they'll teach you to play,
In the dance of the settled, they brighten the day.

Symbiosis in Silence

Two little buddies, a fungus and plant,
Sharing their lunch, no need to rant.
One grows so tall, while the other stays small,
Together in silence, they conquer it all!

In shadows they giggle, beneath the tall trees,
Trading their secrets on a soft summer breeze.
One says to the other, 'You take the best light,'
While the other just chuckles, 'And you keep me white!'

When trouble comes knocking, they hold up their walls,
A fortress of friendship that never just falls.
In silence they flourish, their bond ever tight,
In a world so chaotic, they find pure delight!

So if you hear whispers when strolling outside,
Know it's nature's duo, with nothing to hide.
With giggles and grins, they quietly grow,
In a dance of existence that only they know.

The Art of Slow Growth

In the race of the world, they take a slow stroll,
Measured and steady, that's their one goal.
While others rush by with their frantic pace,
These pals take their time, and they own the place.

With patience like turtles, they stretch out their limbs,
Sipping on sunlight, they leap to their whims.
Watching the clock with a chuckle and grin,
Growing ten inches while you're just thinkin'!

'Why hurry?' they say, as they wiggle in cheer,
'Each inch is a victory, no need for fear!'
And while others grow tall, like they're in a spurt,
These slowpokes know well that sweet patience won't hurt.

So cherish the moments, let laughter abide,
In the art of slow growth, enjoy the ride.
Because when they do flower, oh what a sight,
A masterpiece formed with no rush in the light!

Learning to Cling

On granite cliffs, they hold on so tight,
A twisty embrace, what a comical sight!
With fingers of green, they giggle and sway,
Testing their grip like it's some grand ballet.

'You hang over there, I'll stretch over here!'
Like acrobats tangled, they show no fear.
A tug of the wind makes them laugh with glee,
Who'll win this tug-o-war? Just wait and see!

With patience and flair, they learn their soft ways,
Training for life in the sun's melting rays.
Each hold is a lesson, a new crazy game,
In the world of the clingy, it's all just the same!

So next time you see them, all snug side by side,
Remember their antics, their wild joyful ride.
For in every little grip, they teach us to cling,
To the laughter of life, oh what fun it can bring!

www.ingramcontent.com/pod-product-compliance
Lightning Source LLC
Chambersburg PA
CBHW070750220426
43209CB00083B/379